Quotations of

CHAIRMAN JESSE

We offer here, without comment, the public words of Minnesota's governor, Jesse Ventura. Publication of these quotations is, of course, not "authorized." To require authorization to report the words and deeds of a public official would be to render meaningless the constitutional principles of a free and independent press and an informed electorate.

Quotations of
CHAIRMAN JESSE

Compiled by Myron Rupp

Ruminator Books
St. Paul, Minnesota

Published by Ruminator Books
1648 Grand Avenue
Saint Paul, MN 55105
www.ruminator.com

ISBN: 1-886913-39-0
LCCN: 00-130443

10 9 8 7 6 5 4 3 2 1
First Edition

Photograph by Jonathan D. Chapman
Cover design by Randall Heath
Book design by Wendy Holdman
Typesetting by
Stanton Publication Services
Distributed by
Consortium Book Sales and Distribution

Printed in the United States of America

CONTENTS

I

THE MAKING OF THE MAN
Childhood, Sex Education, and the Navy

II

THE ENTERTAINER
Wrestler, Announcer, Actor, Broadcaster

III

FROM BODY TO MIND
Jesse's Views

IV

THE POLITICAL LIFE

V

THE PRIVATE LIFE

I
The Making
of the Man

"I thank a higher being that my son
wasn't me. And I feel bad for my
mom and dad, because I caused
way more problems than my son
has ever caused me."

"My mother taught us to be very independent, that if we want something, to go out and earn it. Both my mom and dad were always supportive of every crazy idea I ever had."

"My father had seven bronze battle stars in World War II that I never learned about until after he died at age 83. I was with him for 39 years of my life and I never had any idea that this man had seven bronze battle stars. You know how I learned it? My father's [discharge record] was shrunk down in his wallet and I took a magnifying glass and read it."

"It had to do with the fact that in all the 39 years that I knew my dad, he never drove a car. He had a license, but he never drove. My mother drove. And my father's explanation to me was he didn't trust himself."

"[My brother] is very quiet and very to himself. He is the type of person who can't speak in front of 30 people; that would terrify him to death. And yet he can go off and run a marathon and think nothing of it. In his own way he is stronger than I am. And he joined the SEALs before I did . . . And that was how I made it through training—how could I come home, and my parents would say, 'Gee, well, Jan made it and you didn't.'"

"The girl was older than me and she wasn't [a virgin]. So who got seduced?"

"It happened in the state of Nevada.
So it was legal. It still is today. So
I broke no law, right?"

"When I grew up, if you had money and lived in the suburbs, you got to go to college, and didn't have to worry about going to war. But if you were growing up from working class and you had to get a job out of high school, well then you got sent to war. . . . The draft was the most unfair piece of garbage that this country ever put together."

"What the fuck did I do?"

"Just outside the main gate was a mile of road that held something like 350 bars and ten thousand girls, and that was every night. Imagine being nineteen, maybe closing in on twenty, and in the best physical shape of your life. We went out bar-hopping every night."

"It is not that I have a temper to get mad. I get even. I have a vendetta. If I feel someone has wronged me inappropriately, ooh—like all good SEALs, I am very patient about when payback will occur. But it will. (laughs) That's what I think makes us the most dangerous, is the fact that we are very calculating, and we realize that, 'OK, they are on the high roost right now, payback is not going to happen now. But five years down the road, when they least expect it, payback will take place.'"

"I was a twenty-two-year-old freshman, and after four years in the Navy, I'd played man's ultimate game, which is war. There is no way I could view football the way the coaches did—as a life-and-death struggle."

II
The Entertainer

"Win if you can, lose if you must,
but always cheat."

"I'd pose in the ring and tell the crowd, 'Take a look at this body, all you women out there, and then take a look at that fat guy sitting next to you who's eating pretzels and drinking beer. Who would you *really* rather be with?'"

"I will do what I have to do get people down to watch me. If it means saying something to rile the fans, I'll do it. The more people I rile, the more who will pay to see me lose, so the more I'll make myself."

"I bleached my hair blond, because people dislike blond men, especially if they know their hair's been dyed. I wore my hair down to my shoulders and tried my best to look like a surf bum who did nothing but work out on the beach and chase women all day."

"I was the first wrestler to ever
sell out the St. Paul Civic Center.
Nineteen thousand people were
yelling 'Jesse sucks!'"

"I mean, one minute I'm preparing to meet [Hogan] in the Los Angeles Coliseum, and the next minute I'm lying flat on my back fighting for my very existence."

"I haven't wrestled in 12 years. And anyway I'm not some big, dumb wrestler. I know wrestlers who pay more in taxes than most people make. How can they be dumb? Wrestling is ballet with violence. They don't call Nureyev dumb."

THE LESSONS OF WRESTLING

"What did wrestling teach me?
Convince the kids and the adults
will follow."

"When there's money involved, there
ain't no friends."

"You travel a lot—especially to the small towns, the Worthingtons, the Bird Islands. Wrestling is the only pro sport that goes to those places. We call them spot shows, and these are the spot shows of politics. It lets you get the message right out to the people."

Jesse: "What is pain?"

Team: "Pain is weakness leaving the body!"

Jesse: "Pain is good!"

Team: "Extreme pain is extremely good!"

"As long as you're in this state, you
hold no power here. It's very simple.
It's The Body rules. It's my rules or
the highway."

"Do you realize I've kissed Uma
Thurman 17 times? When I did
'Batman and Robin,' she wanted
another take, and I finally put an
end to it."

"It's my show and I can do what
I want. Who said I had to be
responsible?"

III
From Body to Mind

"I've actually changed that moniker.
I'm no longer 'The Body,' I'm Jesse
'The Mind' Ventura."

"Organized religion is a sham and a crutch for weak-minded people who need strength in numbers. It tells people to go out and stick their noses in other people's business."

"Weak-minded doesn't necessarily have to be bad. It means you have a weakness and if . . . going to church will strengthen that mind, then for that person, fine. I'm just speaking on my behalf. I don't have to do it."

"I haven't started any wars
throughout time. Has religion?"

"What's happened in Ireland for
years and years and years? They're
not fighting over potatoes up
there."

"My religious beliefs can be by a lake, they can be on a hill, they can be in the solitude of my own office. And I believe that there's no set example of what people's beliefs should be."

"If I could be reincarnated as a fabric,
I would like to come back as a 38
double-D bra."

"To the best of my knowledge right now, we are at the top of the food chain. So until something comes along and puts us second, you have to accept that. We're the top of the food chain, which means we're going to use resources to survive!"

"If those rules apply, then they ought to be back in birch-bark canoes instead of 200-horsepower Yamaha engines with fish finders. . . . Then it comes back to this: How can one person be allowed to do this and another can't?"

"I'd be happy to pull the switch on a lot of 'em. But boy, if you make a mistake, this is a person's life you're talking about. So, I'm okay with not having it."

"If you're to the point of killing your-
self, and you're that depressed, life
can only get better. If you're a feeble,
weak-minded person to begin with,
I don't have time for you."

"You want to know my definition of gun control? Being able to stand there at 25 meters and put two rounds in the same hole. That's gun control. The gun control people don't know what they're talking about."

"I have no problem with making it
stringent to get them. But I do not
want them taken away and I do not
want them registered. Because
registering—who was the last
great person who registered guns?
Hitler."

"I think that's child abuse . . . because you don't give them the rights of being adults. We need some consistency. We have a hypocrisy. . . . My son had to register for the draft . . . and he can't drink a beer. Now they want to pass a law that you can't buy a gun 'til 21. Yet at 18, they could draft you, give you a gun and send you over to kill people. I don't get that picture."

"These are people who live on the razor's edge and defy death and do things where people die. They're not going to consider grabbing a woman's breast or buttock a major situation. That's much ado about nothing."

"It's the freedom that's important,
  not the symbol."

"There is this bullshit put out there that wealthy people don't pay taxes. That is the standard Democrat, class-warfare approach."

"They tend to be very bullheaded and
noninclusive."

"I don't want to seem hard-core,
but why did you become a parent?
It takes two people to parent. Is it
the government's job to make up for
someone's mistake?"

"If you're smart enough to be here, you're smart enough to get through it. Have we become that dependent on government?"

"Why is everything locked up in the National Archives until the year 2024? See, I believe thoroughly that we killed our own President. And I believe it would destroy the United States for that to be known, and they are just waiting for everyone involved to be dead."

"It's one thing if you want to dally outside your marriage if you go to a motel room, but I have a big problem when it's being done right in the White House, which belongs to us. That's not his house. He is just occupying it. We are the owner, he is the renter, and I think he needs to abide by those rules and show more dignity."

"When he lied to me like that he will
never have credibility again. I will
think: 'Is he telling me the truth or
is he giving me a line of b.s.?'"

"My fault is honesty. When I'm asked
a question, I give an honest answer."

"Prostitution is criminal, and bad things happen because it's run illegally by dirtbags who are criminals. If it's legal, then the girls could have health checks, unions, benefits, anything any other worker gets, and it would be far better."

"It's a lot easier to control something when it's legal than when it's illegal. Nevada don't seem to have a problem with it, do they?"

"I have two friends that have been together forty-one years. If one of them becomes sick, the other one is not even allowed to be at the bedside. I don't believe government should be so hostile, so mean-spirited. . . . Love is bigger than government."

BEING FEATURED IN "DOONESBURY"

"I think that's artistic liberty.
They're enhancing the comic to
better than real life. . . . I'm a public
figure, and they can certainly put
you in a cartoon."

IV
The Political Life

"Keep it simple and stupid."

His philosophy for tackling issues

"My slogan is I'm going to give the neighborhoods back to the neighbors."

"I rode into town, I ran the bad guys
out of town, and now it's time for
me to ride into the sunset with a
hearty 'Hi-yo, Silver.'"

"Aren't we all qualified to serve? I believe that's what our fore-fathers had in mind, that all butchers, bakers, candlestick-makers and former pro wrestlers can all serve."

"I have debated Mr. Coleman and I have debated Mr. Humphrey, and I don't find them any more intelligent than I am. There isn't any reason to think they'd do any better than I would. Hey, if they're so smart and brilliant, they ought to be able to take on an old bumpkin like me."

"Ladies and gentlemen, you cannot legislate stupidity. People are going to do stupid things. We cannot sit and every time someone does something stupid, make it a law and have the government come in, because if you do that, you're going to lose your freedoms."

"Minnesotans know Minnesotans.
You can't take lessons to talk
Fargo."

"(Norm) Coleman? This is a New
Yorker, you remember. He thinks
milk comes from a carton. He's
never even seen a cow."

"Retaliate in '98!"

"I had the first campaign in history
that had an active mosh pit going."

"It ain't over—shall we get sexist—
until the fat lady sings."

"They said a vote for me was a wasted vote. Well guess what? Those wasted votes wasted them."

"Tourism's gonna go up. People are
going to come to Minnesota just to
look at the people who voted me in."

"I've jumped out of an airplane 34 times. I've dove 212 feet under water. I've done a lot of things that defied death. And this isn't defying death. It's just common sense and hard work."

"I can do the job. It's not like it's transplanting kidneys—for that, you get Dr. Najarian. I've got to say, I don't find a lot of elected officials to be all that bright."

"I've never held a job for long, so I may not have a long future in politics."

"It's kind of nice. I plop myself down in the chair, the food comes, and then I can go plop myself down in front of the TV. I don't have to stack the dishwasher. They do it."

"I'm having the time of my life right now! It's nice—when you're governor, you can kind of dictate your own way. I can walk around now and say, 'Jump!' and there are four people who say, 'How high?'"

"I'm not afraid to speak my mind. If I don't get re-elected that's fine. I'll go back to the private sector from whence I came."

"Here we are doing the state's business, with a smile on our faces and laughter in our hearts."

"My brain is operating at such a level that I don't want to put my foot in it."

"I enjoy my relationship with the media, I really do. Because I'm a warrior. And I'm at an age now when I can't go out and be a warrior, so I have to be a mental one. So I've chosen you to be my adversaries."

"You deal with what you need to deal with, I'll deal with what I need to deal with, never the twain shall meet."

"If I were a nightclub singer in
Caesar's Palace, would you ask
the same question?"

"They're dangerous. The media have an agenda. They try to make the public think they're just reporters who report facts. Not true. They carry their personal beliefs and attitudes into the articles they write. I'm a firm believer in free speech, but with any freedom comes responsibility, and the media are abusing their position."

"Judge me by my policies, judge me by my commissioners and judge me by the work that we're trying to do, not a feeding frenzy of media so you can get ratings and make money."

"So for all those naysayers out there who say, 'Oh, the governor shouldn't be standing in front of the cameras, the governor shouldn't be bringing attention to himself,' and all of the stuff that I get, all the crap from the people that don't like me out there—well, this is in your face now, because you all can shut up."

"Who knows, you know? Four years as mayor, then maybe governor, maybe senator or maybe, at the year 2000, Jesse The Body in the White House. Be something to think about."

"I don't have the ego to be the leader
of the free world."

"I would let Gore and Bush hang each other with all the rope they have, to the point where the public can't stand either of them. Their disapproval ratings would skyrocket. Then you enter the race three months before the election and take the whole thing."

"I promised I wouldn't run for president. I never said nothing about the V.P."

"Put your champagne down, we're
going to go dancing right next to
the president and the First Lady
because when the hell might we get
the chance to do it again?"

"She never lived in New York. Why
doesn't she run in Arkansas?
That's where she's from."

V
The Private Life

"FORGET THE DOG.
BEWARE THE OWNER."

The sign above the door
of Jesse Ventura's house

"Why, when you become a public person, do you automatically lose the rights that you have as a citizen? If a homeless person had done to them what I've had done to me, they'd become wealthy with lawsuits."

"There's no rule that says a governor can't have fun. There's no rule that says a governor on his own time can't be a human."

"The perception is that people need to be professional politicians and that therefore being a politician is your entire life. Well, it's not Jesse Ventura's entire life, and I think I was elected upon the fact that I came from being a private citizen."

"Minneapolis. Well, I was born in
Minneapolis. And, besides, have
you ever been to St. Paul? Whoever
designed the streets must have
been drunk. . . . In St. Paul, there's
no rhyme nor reason. It's not
numerical. It's not alphabetical.
I think it was those Irish guys,
you know what they like to do."

"It is already in my will that I will
have 'Stairway To Heaven' play [at
the funeral]. I also love 'Sympathy
For the Devil' by the Rolling Stones,
simply because of the beat and the
lyrics. I love Bob Seger's 'Turn The
Page,' because it very much reminds
me of the years I spent wrestling."

"I love reading real murder mysteries.
Bugliosi; I've read *Helter Skelter*
seven times."

"Haven't read none of the top 10
(on the list of the best 100 novels
of the 20th Century). The ones
I read were because I had to.
Where's Thunderball by Ian Fleming?
Goldfinger? We're just not that
well-read, shall we say?"

"When they get a computer that you simply talk to, then I'll be very into it. But see, when you never learn how to type, you can still do pretty good at it, but you can't hold the good conversations in the chat rooms because you're very illiterate."

104 ★ Quotations of Chairman Jesse

"I've always been attracted to brunettes more than blondes. I enjoy women whose bodies are real. I don't care for the ones who have had breast enhancements and their lips done."

"Have you seen my wife? I don't need
to look for an intern."

"I am cool. Mentally, I'm still 21 or 22 in a lot of ways."

"I see myself closest to Abraham
Lincoln. We're alike in many ways.
We were both wrestlers. And we're
both six-foot four."

"When I get up in the morning, all
I have to do is brush my teeth and
know how good looking I am."

"With those you can be far more
daring and you can do wild things,
and it can bring out in me what I
need now and then to defy death."

"I don't think you'll see as much of it.
You know, I think as you get older
you get more mellow. . . . You don't
settle things physically anymore.
We all go through times in our life
when we settle things physically."

"I consider 'wealth' to be able to go
into a restaurant and order what
you want. And I've achieved that."

"Ten years from now I want to have
my hair grown out long, have a full
beard, have virtually hardly any
material possessions. I want to be
living on a beach on Kona and not
own a watch."

JESSE ON _____

JESSE ON _____

JESSE ON _____

JESSE ON _____

JESSE ON _____

JESSE ON _____

JESSE ON _____

JESSE ON _____

JESSE ON _____

REFERENCES

1. Britt Robson, *City Pages*, 9/30/98
3. David Hanners, *St. Paul Pioneer Press*, 7/19/98
4. Robson
5. Robson
6. Robson
7. Conrad deFiebre, *Minneapolis Star Tribune*, 5/15/99
8. Terry M. Neal, *Washington Post*, 7/7/99
9. Jake Tapper, *Body Slam: The Jesse Ventura Story*
10. Tapper
11. Kevin Dockery and Bill Fawcett (Editors), *The Teams: An Oral History of the U.S. Navy Seals*
12. Robson
13. Tapper
15. Steve Lopez, *Time*, 1/18/99
17. Tapper
18. Tapper
19. Tapper
20. Hanners

21. Pat Doyle and Mike Kaszuba, *Minneapolis Star Tribune*, 1/10/99
22. Matt Bai and David Brauer, *Newsweek*, 11/16/98
23. startribune.com, 12/1/99
24. Hanners
25. Robson
26. Robson
27. Dane Smith, *Minneapolis Star Tribune*, 7/15/99
28. Greg Gordon, *Minneapolis Star Tribune*, 6/4/99
29. Tapper
31. Tapper
33. Lawrence Grobel, *Playboy*, 11/99
34. *Minneapolis Star Tribune*, 10/9/99
35. Robert Whereatt, Conrad deFiebre and Dane Smith, *Minneapolis Star Tribune*, 10/1/99
36. cnn.com, 10/3/99
37. cnn.com, 10/3/99
38. Grobel
39. Laura McCallum, news.mpr.org, 9/11/98
40. wcco.com, 2/21/99
41. Terry M. Neal, *Washington Post*, 2/20/99

42. Grobel

43. Grobel

44. Laura McCallum, news.mpr.org, 9/1/98

45. Gordon

46. Grobel

47. *Minneapolis Star Tribune*, 6/28/99

48. Robson

49. Garry Wills, *The New York Review of Books*, 8/12/99

50. Neal

51. Paul Gray, *Time*, 11/16/98

52. Robson

53. cnn.com, 11/9/98

54. wcco.com, 2/12/99

55. Whereatt, deFiebre and Smith

56. Grobel

57. Dane Smith, *Minneapolis Star Tribune*, 10/22/98

58. Wills

59. Conrad deFiebre, *Minneapolis Star Tribune*, 12/16/98

61. Lopez

63. Tapper
64. Tapper
65. Dane Smith, *Minneapolis Star Tribune*, 9/6/99
66. Bob von Sternberg and Dane Smith,
    Minneapolis Star Tribune, 10/23/98
67. Gray
68. Bai and Brauer
69. wcco.com, 8/29/98
70. Bai and Brauer
71. wcco.com, 2/22/99
72. Pat Doyle, *Minneapolis Star Tribune*, 11/4/98
73. Pam Belluck, *New York Times*, 11/5/98
74. Lopez
75. Belluck
76. von Sternberg and Smith
77. Wills
78. Matt Bai, *Newsweek*, 2/15/99
79. *City Pages*, 12/2/98
80. Jean McMillan, cnn.com, 10/7/99
81. Bai
82. Bai and Brauer

83. *Minnesota Law and Politics,* 11/99

84. cnn.com, 10/5/99

85. wcco.com, 7/14/99

86. Grobel

87. cnn.com, 10/5/99

88. Dane Smith, *Minneapolis Star Tribune,*
6/26/99

89. *Minneapolis Star Tribune,* 1/10/99

90. *Minneapolis Star Tribune,* 10/9/99

91. Grobel

92. Dane Smith, *Minneapolis Star Tribune,*
5/19/99

93. Tom Hamburger and Greg Gordon,
Minneapolis Star Tribune, 2/23/99

94. cnn.com, 2/22/99

95. Gray

97. Wills

98. wcco.com, 7/14/99

99. wcco.com, 7/14/99

100. wcco.com, 2/24/99

101. Robson

102. Robson
103. Dane Smith, *Minneapolis Star Tribune*, 9/6/99
104. Max Rust, *The Minnesota Daily Online*, 12/2/99
105. Grobel
106. Wills
107. Bai and Brauer
108. Richard L. Berke, *New York Times*, 9/19/99
109. Bob von Sternberg, startribune.com, 11/18/98
110. Tapper
111. Doyle and Kaszuba
112. Doyle and Kaszuba
113. startribune.com, 12/1/99